CA$H IN ON YOUR SKILLS

WAYS TO
MAKE MONEY
WRITING

ANGIE TIMMONS

Enslow Publishing
101 W. 23rd Street
Suite 240
New York, NY 10011
USA

enslow.com

Published in 2020 by Enslow Publishing, LLC
101 W. 23rd Street, Suite 240, New York, NY 10011

Library of Congress Cataloging-in-Publication Data

Names: Timmons, Angie, author.
Title: Ways to make money writing / Angie Timmons.
Description: New York : Enslow Publishing, 2020. | Includes bibliographical references and index.
Identifiers: LCCN 2019021029| ISBN 9781978515611 (library bound) | ISBN 9781978515604 (pbk.)
Subjects: LCSH: Authorship--Vocational guidance--Juvenile literature.
Classification: LCC PN151 .T55 2020 | DDC 808.02--dc23
LC record available at https://lccn.loc.gov/2019021029

Printed in China

To Our Readers: We have done our best to make sure all websites in this book were active and appropriate when we went to press. However, the author and the publisher have no control over and assume no liability for the material available on those websites or on any websites they may link to. Any comments or suggestions can be sent by email to customerservice@enslow.com.

CONTENTS

Introduction

When he was a little boy, Henry Patterson would ask his grandmothers if he could eat sweets before tea, a common late-afternoon meal in his home country of England. They always told him the same thing: "Not before tea!"

Henry dreamed about what it'd be like to have a sweets shop. He came up with a story about Pip and Sherb, a mouse and an owl who live in a candy shop called Not Before Tea—inspired by his own experiences as a child who just wants a treat before dinner. He began writing a story in which Pip, the mouse, tries to be helpful around the store. In 2014, at just nine years old, he published the book, *The Adventures of Sherb and Pip: Pip Gets a Job*, through the company he started that same year (Not Before Tea, a children's lifestyle brand based on the book) with the help of grant money. The book sold thousands of copies and his company was very successful. In 2018, the career advice website CareerAddict.com listed Henry as one of the world's top nine most successful teen entrepreneurs.

As a pre-teen, Henry did the hard work to make his dreams come true. He didn't believe other people his age should have to wait until adulthood to begin pursuing their passions, but he also realized most

By age ten, England's Henry Patterson was a published author. He spent his early teenage years growing his own business and working to inspire other young entrepreneurs.

people his age aren't educated about business. So, in 2018, he published *Young and Mighty*, a book aimed specifically at young people who want to pursue their passions, but have little knowledge of how to get started or how to handle the financial aspects of entrepreneurship. He also set up a site for young entrepreneurs, youngmighty.com.

Henry is part of a growing movement in which young people aspire to make money their own way rather than settling into traditional jobs. Young people also increasingly prefer the nature of work in a "gig economy," wherein people work short-term contract or freelance jobs—categories under which many writing jobs fall.

There are many ways to make money through writing, even for teenagers. Many magazines, newspapers, and websites feature content written by teenagers; in fact, some feature content exclusively from teen contributors. These young writers may pen lifestyle columns, cover events for local publications, and review music, movies, and books.

Writing doesn't have to be confined to publications or on web-based sites like blogs. Writers are needed in almost every field, from traditional news jobs to script writing or writing narratives for video games. Identifying early on what kind of writer you'd like to be can fast-track your career by helping you identify what coursework you might need in order to qualify for jobs and by helping you zero in on relevant opportunities you can pursue right now. Though finding your way to a writing career isn't always as clear cut as in other professions, what matters is recognizing you like to write—and how you'd like to cash in on your writing skills.

Tutor Time

I n any attempt to make money, you need to know what you're good at and what you like to do. Equally important is determining what you're not good at and what you don't like to do. In this process, examine your strengths and weaknesses. Start by considering what classes you most enjoy and in which you earn high grades. Also reflect on how well you get along with your peers. If your favorite classes involve writing or language skills and you work well with other students, you might be able to make money by tutoring students who need help in writing or language arts.

Start at School

If tutoring sounds interesting to you, the first step is to check whether your school has a peer-to-peer tutoring system already in place. There are many places where you can tutor other students in writing, but the easiest place to start is in your own school. Tutoring usually takes place on school property, during lunch breaks, free periods, or after school. Some peer tutoring programs operate

Tutoring is a great way to earn money by sharing your writing skills to help someone else improve their writing.

only for academic credit, and you might participate as part of a class in your schedule. But some schools pay students to tutor other students. Even in a program that does not offer payment, tutoring other students can give you valuable experience. You can use this experience to apply to other, paying tutoring services or to start your own.

When you ask to become a writing tutor, the school will probably look at your academic record to see if your grades are good in English and writing and whether you have received any awards or honors for writing. You may have to fill out an application and get recommendations from teachers.

Once you have been accepted into your school's tutoring program, you will be assigned a student or

As a tutor, you'll be assigned to work with students who will need help with their work, such as developing and improving drafts of their written assignments.

students to work with. The school may have a set of skills for you to teach, or you may assist students with specific class assignments. Typically, a student brings a rough draft of a paper or an essay, and you go through it together to identify what works and what doesn't. The student then revises it and brings it back to the next session.

Never rewrite papers for the students you tutor. Remember, you're there to help them improve their own skills by sharing your own. Give them useful feedback to help them see what would improve their writing and what mistakes they should avoid. This strengthens their academic skills and yours!

Tutoring can benefit you in ways other than money. Arif S., who worked as a peer tutor in his school, wrote in *Teen Ink*, "It is a wonderful experience that not only gives a person the satisfaction of teaching another, but it also helps the student more than a teacher sometimes would. Teaching another person something also encourages the peer tutor to be patient, understanding, and sensitive to the student's needs."

You can also tutor students independently outside your school. However, you may find it difficult to get started with new clients if you've never tutored before and lack experience and recommendations.

THE PLAGUE OF PLAGIARISM

Plagiarism, in which people steal others' content and pass it off as their own, is a serious blight on the field of writing. As a tutor, avoid writing assignments for students, even if they offer to pay you. Plagiarism can haunt writers for a long time by seriously damaging their reputations. At school, plagiarism may end up on your permanent record and affect your college and career opportunities.

Plagiarism is a serious offense in the world of writing. As a tutor, ensure you're helping your student be a better writer and not a plagiarist.

The internet has increased instances of plagiarism. Look for plagiarism warning signs, like sudden improvements in a student's writing or content that doesn't quite follow an assignment's guidelines. If you suspect plagiarism, search for pieces of the content on an internet search engine. If it's clear the writing isn't original, confront the student and discuss it with his or her parents or a teacher.

Remember: plagiarism is never worth the consequences.

If you are in this situation, you might try tutoring as a community service. This can build your reputation and earn personal recommendations from students and parents.

Off School Grounds

You've tutored your peers through the school's tutoring program, either as a class or for community service, and you may have even made some money doing so. Now, you'd like to make money tutoring outside the school system. Many companies hire students to tutor other students. If you have built up your résumé with school tutoring experience, you'll be in good shape to apply to one of these tutoring companies. Your résumé should include your grades and academic honors, as well as your school tutoring experience. Also important are recommendations from your students, teachers, and the administrator who oversees the school's tutoring program. If you have been tutoring privately, include references from your students and their parents. The more proof you have of your effectiveness as a tutor, the more likely you are to be hired by a tutoring company.

Once you have your references and résumé ready, find tutoring companies that operate in your area and contact them. Call and ask to speak to the manager to ask if the company is hiring writing tutors. Discuss your experience and expertise in writing. Find out if the company hires teen tutors or only adults with college degrees or classroom teaching experience. If the company does employ teens, you will probably be required to fill out an application for employment and to go for an in-person interview. If the company requires your academic transcript for review, you can request this from your school's guidance counselor.

If the manager tells you that the company does not have any current openings, ask if you can send in your résumé to keep on hand for future job openings. It's also a good idea to get the name and contact information of the person in charge of hiring so that you can communicate with him or her directly. Check back with the company on a regular basis to see if it has any openings and to make sure that your name and information remain on the top of the pile.

There are also online tutoring companies, many of which hire teens to tutor other teens. These companies may have more students in need of tutors since they aren't limited to just one geographic location.

Entrepreneurial Tutoring

Perhaps you've tutored for your school and then for a local tutoring company, and you feel that you have enough experience to start your own tutoring service. You may even decide to hire other student tutors to work for you, especially if you want to broaden your tutoring to other subjects besides writing and need teens with different academic expertise. You can advertise your services locally, both in schools and in the community. If you charge slightly lower rates than local tutoring companies, you can attract your own clientele.

Erik Kimel started his own private tutoring business in the suburbs of Washington, DC, when he was a senior in high school. He started his business, Peer2Peer Tutors, in 2004 with an ad in the local paper that read, "Students learn best from other students. Any subject. Any grade. Call Erik." His $50 newspaper ad kicked off a company that Kimel continued to run through college and beyond. According to the company's LinkedIn page, the company had created five thousand jobs for young people, served as many students, and provided one-hundred thousand hours of tutoring through its multiple locations across the United States in its fifteen-year existence.

Peer-to-Peer Possibilities

While tutoring teens or younger students in writing can be a good way to make money, be wary of some possibilities. Working with peers your own age can be challenging, especially if a student doesn't want tutoring, but has been forced into it. You must create a working relationship that includes good communication and trust to get results. Try to find a shared interest or come to an agreement about goals and how you can best work together. Tutoring may result in a friendship, but not always. If you encounter difficulty getting your student to cooperate or make progress in a school setting, enlist the help of a parent, a teacher, or an administrator. At a tutoring company, seek help from your supervisor.

Using your writing skills to tutor other students can be a profitable way to take advantage of something you do well while helping other students who have more trouble. But just as teaching isn't for everyone, tutoring may not be what you want to do. Now, let's look at ways to help you reach a wider audience with your writing.

Journalism: From Who to How

Nearly every town has a local newspaper. Smaller and mid-sized towns may have a weekly newspaper, while larger towns and cities often have at least one daily newspaper. Many towns and cities also have magazines, television news, radio news, and web-based news run either by a news organization or community or civic organization. Chances are, your school has a newspaper and perhaps even a journalism club. All these media outlets provide multiple opportunities to use your writing skills in the field of journalism.

The Essential Questions

Before you start looking for writing opportunities with a local newspaper, it helps to understand some of the basic elements of journalism.

Writing an article or a story for a newspaper involves some very basic questions: Who? What? When? Where? Why? How? These are the questions readers want answered when they read an article in their local paper, no matter what the subject is. Any

If your school has a student newspaper, sign up to write for it. You'll learn valuable journalistic skills and perhaps other skills.

newspaper story should answer these questions, even if it's just about a school basketball game or theater performance.

In reporting "hard" news, such as stories about crimes or other important events, the article is usually arranged in what is called the inverted pyramid style. This means that the most important part of the story comes first (for example, what disaster occurred), followed in declining order of importance by the other elements of the story (whether people were

All news stories should address six questions in order to be considered complete: Who, What, When, Where, Why, and How.

killed or injured, the extent of property damage, the nature of the emergency response, etc.). These elements should answer the basic questions asked above. It is also important to answer the question "So what?" Explain why readers should be interested in or care about the story.

GATEKEEPERS AND WATCHDOGS

Journalists are often referred to as the "gatekeepers" of our society because reporters, editors, and news producers (for television and radio news) decide what stories to cover, who to interview, and what sources to use. That means the public is exposed to what those people decide is newsworthy. This is a very serious responsibility that should be undertaken with the public's best interest at heart.

Another term for journalists is "watchdogs" because they are entrusted as truth seekers responsible for keeping an eye on those in power—like elected officials and others who wield a lot of influence. Being a good watchdog entails keen observational and research skills and a strong desire to hold those in power accountable to the people who put them there.

If you like the idea of being a truth champion for the public, your writing skills will be put to good use in journalism.

Above all, a news piece must capture the reader's interest, meaning all of this must be written in a way that's colorful and interesting as well. To enliven a story, journalists usually add "human interest" elements such as interviews, opinions, and eyewitness accounts.

Finally, since journalists are expected to report the truth, the story must be told in a way that is fair and balanced.

Start Local

So, you're comfortable with the kind of writing that is required for newspapers. Now you'd like to find some opportunities to do this type of writing and get paid for it. The first thing to do is to start reading your local newspaper regularly. Are any reporters regularly covering school news, school sporting events, and other school activities? Does it appear to be the same person who writes all these stories? Is there a regular piece written by a student? If you don't see a student-written column—or any items specifically about students and schools—then propose this coverage.

Examine student-written features in other newspapers, which you can often access online. As you read these pieces, you'll get a sense of what students generally write for newspapers and how

To get an idea of what you might be able to offer your local newspaper, read it regularly to see what it already covers and what it's missing.

you can do the same for your local paper. Print some of these columns or clips to show what is possible in a student-written feature.

Meet the Editors

The people who make decisions about a newspaper's content is the editor in chief and/or section editors, depending on the size of the publication. You can usually find their names on the newspaper's masthead (where the names of the publication's owners and staff are found) or on the website. These are the people you should contact. Call or email to ask if you can make an appointment to discuss the possibility of writing for the paper. Be sure to mention that you are a student. Also remember to be as professional as possible.

You should go into your meeting with the editor with a specific idea of what your story or column would cover. Would it focus on school news? Sports? Extracurricular activities? Special events? School-to-community issues? How often would it print? Have a serious, specific proposal.

Editors will want to know what kind of writing experience you have. If you have been a part of your school's newspaper or journalism club, you can show that you have the necessary experience. Use any kind of writing experience to persuade the editor that you can handle a regular weekly or biweekly writing job. If you have clips (samples of your writing) from a school paper, provide those. If you do not, try writing a sample column or story as if you already had the job. Show the editor how well you write.

Digital News

Today, most newspapers publish not only a print version of the publication, but also an online version as well. Because online content is not limited by the costs of paper and printing, there is usually more room for additional information, stories, features, and departments (recurring sections in publications like magazines and newspapers). If your local newspaper cannot spare any room in its print version for a student-written department, ask the editor if he or she would be willing to develop one in the online version.

Interns and Correspondents

Perhaps you have great ideas and a good writing style, but the editor still turns you down. What can you do now? You can ask if the paper has any internship opportunities. As an intern, you can work for the paper part-time, often without pay, to gain skills and learn the business. This can often lead to writing for the paper or even to a regular job.

Another option is to become a stringer, a newspaper correspondent who is not part of a regular newspaper staff, but is hired on a part-time basis to report on events. Small newspapers may not have the money for someone to write a regular piece

Even if they don't pay, internships are a great way to gain real-world, professional writing experience that can help you land paid writing work in the future.

about school-related matters, but still need someone to report on school events or meetings. This is a great way to gain experience with basic reporting.

Professionalism in Journalism

If you do find yourself with a regular feature in a newspaper or you have been given an internship or stringing opportunity, you should always present a professional appearance in public. Dress neatly, avoiding casual clothing. Pay attention instead of talking, texting, or fooling around on your cell phone; in fact, turn your cell phone on silent when you're conducting an interview or covering a meeting or event. Listen respectfully to the people you interview. Be prepared so you can ask intelligent questions. If you are all-around professional, you'll earn the trust of the people you interact with and work for.

What's Next?

If you've been working as a stringer, intern, or regular contributor, the editorial staff may decide you can have your own feature. The editor will then have a clear set of expectations for what your feature will include, how frequently it will appear, and what it will cover.

Your editor will give you a word count to follow so that the feature's length fits the paper. There will also be a strict deadline. The paper may provide a style guide (most newspapers use Associated Press style as well as some guidelines specific to their publications). They also have expectations for verifying sources, what topics to avoid, and other issues. You are responsible for reading and following these guidelines.

Shadowing other reporters may be helpful before you begin your internship, stringing, or regular feature. Ask if you can spend some time with reporters who are sent out to cover a variety of events and conduct a variety of interviews. Observe how they approach sources, get information, and turn it all into a story. An experienced reporter can also show you how to sift through what is accurate versus what is unverifiable information.

The Value of News Experience

Newspaper journalism is a skill that teen writers can use to generate income right now. It can also lead to similar writing at the college level and even in the professional world. It is real-world writing, and if you love to talk to people and be in the thick of the news, it may be the perfect fit for you.

The Online Content Bazaar

Wherever you go online, there's content. With millions of websites on the internet, there's a huge demand for writers to cover a vast array of subjects for hugely diverse audiences who have a variety of interests.

A lot of online content is created by freelance writers. Teens can find multiple money-making opportunities as online freelance writers, especially if they're particularly knowledgeable in popular topics—which, depending on the website and its audience, can be anything from fashion to science fiction. From the comfort of your bedroom, you can make money as an online writer and stock your professional writing portfolio with work samples.

Online Opportunities

There are many sites that need content. The best way to start is to find one set up to purchase content from freelance writers or that connects writers with

Teenagers can find any number of online freelance writing opportunities, such as writing for blogs, lifestyle sites, online stores, and sites dedicated to specific interests or audiences.

opportunities, like Trionds.com, which puts writers together with guest blogging and article-writing freelance work.

If you love to blog, you can set up your own blog. Eva Baker started TeensGotCents.com as part of a

ONLINE CONTENT CONSIDERATIONS

A drawback to writing online content as a teen is that some sites may not hire or pay you until you are eighteen. However, if you're interested in getting your writing out there and building a portfolio of your work, it's worth pursuing web-based writing opportunities—even if they don't pay.

Always have a parent or guardian examine any websites you're considering writing for. Be sure you want your name associated with a particular site. In addition, writers are often required to sign up on a site and establish online payment accounts, such as PayPal, to receive payment. So, it is always best to have an adult check the site for you before you proceed. Some sites also require you to be a certain age before you can contribute content or be paid. Read the fine print so that there won't be unpleasant surprises.

school project when she was just sixteen. Within a couple of years, she was not only making money from her blog, but also getting hired as a speaker and brand ambassador (someone who gets paid by a company to represent a product or promote brand awareness).

You can take more control over what and how often you write with your own blog. With enough traffic, you may be able to monetize your blog.

To make money on your own blog, place pay-per-click advertisements on it to generate income. This is effective only if you blog about something that generates enough interest to lead to many advertising clicks. If you can generate enough readership, advertisers—especially those promoting products related to what you write about on your

With so many websites on the internet, there's always a need for writers who can develop content that keeps followers and new visitors continuously interested.

blog—may approach you about placing their ads on your blog site or giving you financial or product consideration in exchange for mentioning those products.

If the idea of writing articles or blog posts isn't appealing, there are other ways to make money online using your writing skills.

Reviews

There are some websites, like SeedingUp.com and GetReviewed.org, which connect writers with opportunities to get paid to write reviews of various products. (Note that product review sites sometimes don't last very long or may pay very little per review, so research to ensure they're credible and safe to do business with.)

One way to approach review writing is to concentrate on a product you care about and websites that feature content related to that product. Companies selling items like video games, cosmetics, clothing, sports equipment, and software (the list goes on!) need reviews to increase product awareness and sales. Websites devoted to certain subjects, like television shows, book series, or comic books may also pay for reviews.

Consider what you'd like to review and look for sites that support that interest. This is an important consideration for anyone who wants to pursue a writing career in a certain field, like fashion, technology, sports, or entertainment; any writing samples you can produce related to your field of interest, whether you got paid for them or not, will go a long way in making you a credible writing candidate in the future. Hopefully, you can find one

Like writing letters? Some websites hire freelance writers to pen custom letters, some of which can be purchased repeatedly—earning you more money.

or more websites that will pay you for reviews; if not, you can still have fun writing about something you enjoy while building your portfolio of writing samples.

The Lost Art of Letter Writing

With the proliferation of email, social media, text messaging, and other digital messaging, it's been a long time since some people have written formal or professional letters. Others may simply not know where to start in writing a letter that they need for personal or professional use. Sites like WritersPerHour.com connect writers with people willing to pay for anything from love letters to cover letters for job applications. Usually, writers are paid for each custom letter they write, and may receive additional money if that letter is purchased again in the future.

Business Sites

Teen writers can also write online content for local businesses. For example, small businesses like stores and restaurants may have their own websites, but lack the time to continually generate fresh content. Succeeding in this market requires organization and effort on the part of the writer. Constructing a website or creating advertising materials may be necessary to generate business. It can also be worthwhile to visit local businesses and ask if they have a need for this kind of service. When approaching business owners, it is helpful to have a business card and writing samples to share.

Social Media: The New Content Frontier

Social media has shouldered its way into the legitimate content market by proving it's an effective, easy, and affordable way to reach a lot of different

Most young people are already proficient in using social media. Some companies will pay writers to create and post content on their social media channels.

37

audiences in a lot of different places. With everyone from pre-teens to grandparents on social media networks like Facebook, Twitter, and Instagram, writers are increasingly needed by businesses, politicians, interest groups, and other outlets to create social media-specific content.

Large entities usually have marketing departments or consultants who help develop social media content. Some smaller companies, however, may not have the money to hire full-time marketers or writers to create social media content. They might not have the time to create it themselves, either, considering social media is most effective when posted on every day. Therefore, they may hire freelance writers to post regularly on social media for them. If you are very comfortable with social media sites and can write content related to the company's business, this can be a great job.

Regarding Reputation

The internet may be the land of opportunity for writers, but it's also a much smaller world than many people realize. Once something is on the internet, it's on there forever. Remember that any time you put your name to something on the internet, there is a chance that it could come back to haunt you.

Be sure to publish only your best work. Never write anything that you might someday regret. Any piece of writing with your name on it represents you.

Avoid working for websites that pay writers for content that other people will pass off as their own. Remember, plagiarism is a serious offense that can haunt a writer for years.

Worth the Work

The key to making money online as a teen writer is simply hard work. With most content sites, you'll need to write many articles to generate a reasonable amount of money. But if you can commit to spending time every day writing and then posting your articles, you can not only make some money, but also establish yourself as a writer with a visible portfolio. The best part is, you can accomplish this without having to get dressed up or even leave home!

Your Words in Print

There are many ways to write in today's world with internet-based communication methods like blogs and social media. However, many writers still like to see their words on an actual page, such as in a book or in a magazine. Writers who want the chance to see their words in print might consider freelancing, which, while less predictable than full-time writing jobs, can sometimes pay well while also providing the opportunity to write for a variety of publications.

Magazine Freelancing

Freelance writing for magazines follows a certain process. The writer writes a story, article, or poem and then looks for a market where it might be published. Typically, writers can submit their writing in two ways. They can either send in an entire piece of writing, or they can query an editor at a magazine or publishing house. This means they write a letter presenting an idea in the hope that the editor will

Freelance writing is a good way to break in to the writing industry, giving your portfolio a diverse selection of writing samples from different segments of the publishing industry.

like the concept and want to publish the work. If a magazine accepts a piece of writing, it is published months later, as magazines generally work as much as a year ahead of a specific issue. Payment may occur when the piece is accepted or not until it is actually published.

What to Write, and How Often?

For many writers, writing for magazines is a good way to break into the business. A typical magazine must fill its pages with content month after month, or even weekly. This makes the odds of selling your work to a magazine better than selling work to a book publisher because magazines need new content all the time.

Though print media has suffered with the rise of online content, there are still many magazines on the market that feature content on a diverse array of topics and interests.

Magazines also publish a wide variety of content. No matter what subject you're interested in writing about, be it science fiction, gaming, movies, horses, or extreme sports, chances are there's a magazine about it. The content can also take many different forms, from traditional stories and articles to interviews, personal experience pieces, reviews, commentaries, and travelogues (pieces that describe a travel experience or trip). You can choose to write about something you're interested in and then try to sell your piece. Or you can examine a magazine's list of themes for upcoming issues (usually found on the magazine's website) and try to write something to fit a theme. Be sure to give plenty of lead time, as magazines are put together many months before they are actually published.

Magazines also have regular departments or features, but for a teen writer, getting one can be difficult to achieve.

The Magazine Market

If you are interested in developing a freelance writing career with magazines, where do you start? The first thing to do is make a list of magazines that publish writing by teens. You can find many of them online simply by searching for magazines that accept teen writing. You can also use a magazine market guide, available at your local library or bookstore. There are several of these: some are aimed at people who write for children and some are aimed at people who write for adults. Market guides for children's writers usually have a section that specifically discusses markets for young writers.

Whatever guide you decide to use, read through the listings carefully. Note what each magazine

If you want to write for magazines, do your research; visit a library or bookstore to peruse different magazines and find which kind might be a good fit for you.

publishes and whether it accepts work only from writers of a certain age. Some magazines are paying markets and some are not, so you must decide if you're only willing to write for pay or if it's more important to you to create a body of published work.

Find Your Fit

Once you have identified some possible magazine markets for your work, study each magazine and its guidelines for writers. Find magazines at a local library or bookstore. Examine them to see what kind of articles and stories it publishes. Also note the overall tone of the magazine. Are its articles light and funny? Are they written in a casual, or even trendy, style? Or is the magazine serious and formal in presentation and tone? Only by reading a magazine can you get a feel for it and decide whether your writing would fit. It is possible to read parts of some magazines online, but these samples may not give you the complete "flavor" of the magazine. (Of course, if you're thinking of an online-only magazine or e-zine as a market, you should read the entire issue electronically.)

Every magazine has a set of guidelines for potential writers. Magazines specify what kinds of writing they publish, general word counts, and how to submit work to the magazine. It is important to pay attention to these points; otherwise, the chances of the story being accepted are slim. No matter how you send your submission, be sure that it looks as professional as possible.

Teen 'zines

There are some excellent magazine markets for young writers where you can get your first publishing credits. Even though many don't pay young writers for their submissions, they can start you on the path to becoming a professional author. Check each magazine's website and read some sample stories and poems. Ensure that what you plan to submit matches the magazine's style and content. Some good magazine markets for teen writers include:

- *New Moon Girls* (www.newmoon.com). Most of this magazine's content is written by girls, and a team of girls edits the content.
- *Polyphony Lit* (www.polyphonylit.com). A national, student-run literary magazine for high school writers and editors, this publication showcases student fiction, nonfiction, and poetry.
- *Skipping Stones* (www.skippingstones.org). A nonprofit magazine for writers ages eight to

PATIENCE IN PUBLISHING

Once you have submitted a piece to a magazine or a book to a publisher, you must be prepared to be patient. Responses can take a long time, and these days, some magazines or publishers won't respond at all if they decide that your writing isn't a good fit. Resist the urge to call, email, or write to ask about your submission too much, as it is unprofessional and can be annoying to overburdened editors. If you want to make sure that your submission was received, it's acceptable to include a self-addressed, stamped postcard that the editor can easily drop into the mail, letting you know that your work was received.

sixteen, *Skipping Stones* celebrates different cultures.

- *Stone Soup* (stonesoup.com). This magazine contains writing and art by young people ages eight to thirteen.
- *Teen Ink* (www.teenink.com). *Teen Ink* includes a literary magazine, website, and books, all written by teen writers.

A Word About Books

Writing a book and having it published is the ultimate dream of many teen writers. And it might seem like the best way to make a great deal of money quickly. But, there are several reasons why teens don't routinely have books published by traditional book publishers. The primary reason is that a teen's writing simply hasn't matured enough to be published. Even the most promising young writers can look back at their work years later and be critical of their early efforts. Book publishing is

Most writers dream of one day publishing their very own book. While not an impossible dream, it's a competitive and challenging one; therefore, authors are increasingly choosing to self-publish.

also an extremely competitive field, particularly in a poor economy. Publishers want books that are guaranteed to have a large audience, and it is difficult to sell books by unknown teen writers. Many book publishers won't even consider work by teen authors for these reasons.

Self-Publishing

Self-publishing is increasingly popular, and it may seem like an easy way to turn your work into a book. However, it can be difficult to actually make any money with a self-published book. Because these books have a reputation for uneven quality, many bookstores are reluctant to carry them. And unless you are prepared to spend a great deal of time promoting and marketing your book, it is unlikely that you will sell very many copies. Most self-published books only ever sell a few hundred copies at most, even though they may be available on sites like Amazon and Barnes & Noble. And as self-publishing proliferates, it will likely become even more difficult to get your book noticed.

Freelancing Facts

As a way to earn money, traditional freelance writing can be very hit or miss, since you must first create a piece and then find a place to sell it. The process is similar in book publishing, which can be even more difficult. Because books are long and expensive to publish, book editors must be very choosy.

Many writers believe that shorter pieces of writing, such as those intended for magazines, are a good way to hone writing skills and build a body of published work. These samples can come in handy later when submitting query letters to book publishers. Freelance writing for print may be tougher than online content writing, and often more frustrating, but the satisfaction of seeing your words on a physical page is hard to beat.

The Next Chapter

Whether you're heading into a new year in high school, heading off to college, or entering the working world, hopefully you've gotten a start on your money-making writing career. You may have accomplished this by tutoring, freelancing, or even setting up your own blog or self-publishing, like young Henry Patterson. How do you put all the pieces together to convince the next decision-maker, whether that person is a college admissions professional, editor, or hiring manager, that you've got what it takes?

Show Off

You've got terrific writing skills, and you've accumulated published clips and know how to work with editors or clients. All these things can help you write a great college application essay and hopefully win you acceptance at the school of your choice. If you hope to major in creative writing or journalism, you can use some of your published clips as part of your application.

Maintaining a portfolio, either digital or physical (preferably both!), of your writing samples is necessary to show potential clients, employers, and even colleges that you're a skilled writer.

Many college courses are heavily dependent on writing, so your honed writing skills will help you move through your college years more easily.

Collegiate Writing

Being a fluid and skillful writer will help with your overall academic success. You can also continue to use your skills to make money while you're in

WRITING WITH STYLE

Most writing jobs require adherence to specific style guidelines that are often set forth in style guides, like the *Associated Press Handbook* or the *Chicago Manual of Style*. These style guides, which can be found at your library or online, dictate rules about everything from punctuation to citing sources.

Most writing jobs also have rules about formatting for things like spacing and fonts. When you get a writing job, ask what the editor prefers in terms of formatting so you can get it right the first time. Avoid fancy fonts and using font colors that aren't black. If submitting a piece in printed form, print only on one side of the paper for ease of reading and editing. Remember: editors read for a living. Do yourself and them a favor by making your work easy on the eyes.

college. Most colleges have writing centers where students can go for help with papers and essays. With strong writing skills and experience, you have a good chance of being hired to work there and tutor other college students. If you've found success with freelance writing and online content development, those are also easy to continue while you're in college. You can adjust your freelance writing workload based on how much time your academic work takes and how much time you are willing to allot for your paid writing.

If journalism is the type of writing you enjoy most, you can join your college's newspaper or yearbook, or even contribute to its websites.

No matter what path you decide to take in college and beyond, your experience making money with writing, and the way you've polished your writing skills, will serve you well. Almost every type of business needs people who communicate well in writing. For example, if you decide to pursue marketing as a career, your skills can help you with commercial copywriting. Strengthening your writing skills early on helps set the stage for future success.

Student Interns

As a high school student and especially as a college student, one way to gain experience in writing

You might be able to make money tutoring others in writing after high school; most colleges have writing centers that help students with their writing assignments.

CALL FOR COPYWRITERS

Lots of jobs fall under the umbrella of copywriting. For instance, technical writers (who write instructional and/or educational copy) are always needed in businesses as varied as technology and human resources. The field of technical writing is diverse, and technical writers are almost always in demand.

Politicians, candidates, and public figures also need copywriters to help them write speeches, website and social media content, and position statements. See if anyone locally can use a campaign writer.

Marketing is another field that always needs writers because as an industry, it has a huge scope. Marketing writers who can develop anything from proposal to website content are often sought by marketing departments within companies or by agencies devoted solely to marketing.

Freelancers can find a lot of copywriting opportunities through a simple internet search. Refine the search by adding the field (like technical, political, or marketing) you'd most like to work in.

and publishing is through an internship. Many publishing companies offer internships to students. They may not be paid positions, but for several months during the school year or summer break you can help put together a magazine or see how books are created. You may even get the chance to have your writing published in a magazine or on a website, under your byline, which is a great way to start building a portfolio. Most publishers' websites tell you if they accept interns and explain how to apply for these positions.

Go for the Win

There are many contests that recognize the work of talented teen writers. Categories include fiction, nonfiction, essays, opinion pieces, and more. Some organizations actually hand out cash prizes for winning writing, and others award scholarships. While some contests just offer publication, winning them gets your writing into the public eye and looks impressive on your résumé or in your portfolio. Search online to see what contests are out there and how you can enter.

Use Your Skills to Give Back

Remember that applying your writing skills can be about more than just making money. Perhaps you'd like to share your writing skills with people who need them, simply as a community service or as a way to contribute to a cause that you believe in. Many nonprofit organizations need good writers to help them. Volunteering gives you the opportunity to share your skills for a good cause and also add to your résumé of published work. Are you interested in organizations that work for human rights, environmental advocacy, animal protection, or other issues? Is there a homeless shelter or food pantry near you? These kinds of organizations may

Charities need all kinds of help, including from writers who can help create content like newsletters, fundraising emails, social media posts, and other literature.

need someone to write a newsletter for them, but they may not be able to afford to pay a writer to do it. They may need someone to update their Facebook page on a regular basis or create email news reports. These are all excellent opportunities for using your writing skills and benefitting the community at the

Many successful businesspeople also use their skills in charitable ways. Look for ways you can do good with your writing skills at places like nursing homes or community centers.

same time.

Do you belong to a church, synagogue, mosque, or other religious group? Are you a member of a youth group? Perhaps you can use your writing skills to start a members' newsletter. Or you might contribute to an existing newsletter with articles about young people and their activities. If you are part of a local dance troupe, theater group, or musical performance group, it might need someone to write press releases or promotional materials. And don't forget that you can use your writing and tutoring skills to work with underprivileged children for free. There are many ways to use your writing skills as a volunteer, and you'll make a solid contribution as well as continue to build your own skills and portfolio.

Preparing for the Business Side of Things

Writers have long depended on others for opportunities and success (publishers who may not ever have a chance to look at your manuscripts, editors who control what they're willing to publish or air, hiring managers looking for writers), but young entrepreneurs like Henry Patterson are breaking down those barriers. They're doing so by making their own rules, like self-publishing and applying their entrepreneurial spirit to grow their own brands. While stories like Patterson's certainly aren't the norm, they can serve as an inspiration for anyone who doesn't want to wait until college, adulthood, or their first "real job" to begin writing their own stories—literally and figuratively!

What it comes down to is this: If you love to write, you can use your skills and your enthusiasm for the craft of writing to earn income and contribute to your community. People who make money doing what they love to do are the luckiest people of all.

The Business of Writing Entrepreneurship

Every business, even freelance writing that you do from the comfort of your couch, is guided by certain expectations. It is, after all, business, and making good impressions is absolutely critical. Knowing what to expect in the writing business can help you tremendously as you set out to cash in on your writing skills.

Basic Rules of Professionalism

There are some basic rules to follow in formatting and submitting professional writing. Maybe you're used to writing longhand, with pencil or pen on paper. This might be fine for brainstorming a first draft, but you should never submit anything handwritten to an editor or publisher. Submitting work via email, which is increasingly common, makes it almost impossible to send handwritten stories or

In everything from how you present yourself physically to how you organize your time and submit your writing, be professional. Reputation goes a long way in the writing world.

articles. However, some companies still accept manuscripts via regular mail. Avoid sending handwritten materials.

If you're used to writing on a computer, you may assume the computer's spelling and grammar check programs will catch mistakes. However, you can't rely on these tools because they don't always catch everything, like words that are spelled correctly, but used incorrectly. Sometimes it autocorrects words, changing them into something unintended. Proofread your writing before submitting it. Not only should you proofread it right after you finish writing, but also after letting it "cool" for a day or two. You'll be amazed at what you might have missed the first time.

Write the Right Way

An important aspect of becoming a professional writer has to do with etiquette. You need to use your best manners in your dealings with editors, publishers, clients, peers, and anyone else you encounter as a writer. Remember, you are starting a business, and it's vital to act in a professional, businesslike way. Pay careful attention to deadlines and treat them as unbreakable. Don't tell

Deadlines go hand-in-hand with nearly every writing job. Your reputation, as well as the outlets for which you write, depend on meeting deadlines.

63

yourself you have plenty of time only to end up scrambling at the last moment. That is a stressful situation that can result in poorly written content. Try to finish submissions with a few days to spare; that will help build your reputation with clients and result in more future business.

Expectations

Remember to act like a professional in your interactions with editors and clients, too. Respect the ways that people want to be contacted. Communicate clearly and appropriately. If you're submitting to a magazine as a freelance writer, you should not call or email incessantly to check the status of your submission. As long as you have included all of your contact information, editors will get in touch with you if they are interested in publishing your work. And remember the truth in submitting as a freelance writer: No news generally means "No." If you don't hear back about a submission after a few months, it most likely means the editor is not interested in the piece.

Writing Rates

Some of the publications you might write for, such as online content sites or magazines, will have set payment rates. They may calculate their rates per word written, or for the entire writing project. But

Tracking the time you spend writing is important to help you understand how long different projects take you to complete, set rates, or report what you're owed per hour.

some clients may ask what your rate is per hour of writing. The best way to handle this is to find out what other writers are charging for similar work and then set your rate accordingly. Remember, as a teen it's a good idea to set your rates lower than those of more seasoned professional writers to attract the business you need to build up your new business and future career.

It is also important to keep track of the time you spend writing. Most writing is done for a set rate, regardless of the time spent, but some companies expect you to charge according to the number of hours you worked on a writing project. As you track your progress on different projects, you should record the exact number of hours you spend on each. Even if you aren't being paid an hourly rate, it will help you establish just how long different kinds of projects take you to complete. This will help you get a sense of how much you are earning for your time and will help you plan for future projects.

Work, Clients, Money: Keeping Track

An important aspect of being a professional writer is keeping track of your work. You need to create a tracking system for all your submissions and assigned work. That way you'll know, for example, if you submitted a piece to a publication so long ago that you can assume it was rejected. Then you can send it somewhere else.

Spreadsheets work well for keeping track of what you have sent out, when you sent it, and to whom you sent it. They also work well for keeping track of assigned work. Create a chart that lists the writing

If you're contemplating starting a writing business, familiarize yourself with software like Excel spreadsheets or Google Sheets where you can track your assignments, due dates, hours, and finances.

you have been assigned, when it is due, and where it should be sent. By checking these spreadsheets daily, you'll always have a clear picture of what is due and what you have finished.

Get Paid

Keep track of payments and do not rely on various publications or businesses to make sure that you are paid. For every piece of writing that you sell, list the date of the invoice (bill) and the payment amount due to you. Then check it off when it has been paid. You may want to create an invoice template for clients that don't have their own invoices. You can adjust the template for the job you are doing.

At first, you may not earn enough in a year of writing to need to file taxes, but if you do, your payment spreadsheet will also be a clear record of what you earned and from whom. Any time you receive payment, keep the check stub or a printout or PDF of the payment history from a source such as PayPal, as a record of your earnings. Keep these filed in a safe place.

Written Agreements for Writers

Eventually, most writers will have to sign a contract for a specific piece of writing. A contract is a formal agreement between the writer and the organization buying the writing. It spells out exactly what is expected of both of you. The contract usually addresses the question of rights to the work. When you sell a piece of writing, you are selling someone the rights to use that writing, but the nature of these rights can vary. Ask an adult like a teacher for help understanding contracts, if necessary. Make sure you fully grasp the language used in the contracts.

It might be tempting to ask for more money or different rights when you're given a contract to sign. Obviously, if you feel the terms are unfair, you should try to work out something else. But be aware that when you are just starting out in your writing career, it can be more important to get your writing in print for your portfolio than it is to argue over payment and rights. You run the risk of having the editor say, "Never mind."

Advertising

As a writer starting a business, you need to advertise your services. This can be as simple as using your computer to create business cards and a brochure of the services you offer. If you have enough experience, you can create a résumé that lists what you have written and what companies you have worked for. You can find résumé templates online or through software like Microsoft Word, as well as other materials such as business cards and advertisements. You can also get the help of a local printing company if you want to spend more money.

It's important that you present yourself professionally in your advertising. Stay away from cutesy images, distracting fonts, or phrases like "aspiring author." Include your name, address, email, phone number, and website if you have one. Plain and simple is best.

Putting It All Together

Put together a portfolio of your best published work. This can be a file folder or a loose-leaf binder with plastic page protectors or a digital portfolio that you set up on a website or keep in electronic form. Portfolios allow prospective clients to browse through your work. Some book and magazine editors require "clips" with a submission or query. A clip is simply a copy of anything that you've written and published professionally. You can access these from your portfolio when you need to. You should also keep some of your clips in digital format so that they can be attached to an email submission easily. (If necessary, you can digitize print documents with the help of a scanner.)

Becoming a professional writer is an exciting process, but it does take work. You want to do everything you can to advertise yourself and create a solid reputation. After all, this is your business!

GLOSSARY

client A person or group that receives the professional services of an individual or business.

contract A written agreement between two or more parties that is legally binding.

digital Technology that supports electronic communications over the internet and electronic versions of things like portfolios.

editorial A piece in a newspaper or periodical that presents the opinion of the publisher or editorial board.

entrepreneur Someone who starts and runs his or her own business rather than working for another person.

etiquette Conventional rules for proper social behavior.

e-zine An electronic (internet) magazine.

feature A newspaper or magazine article devoted to in-depth coverage of a special topic, usually not tied to breaking news.

freelance To sell work or services by the hour or by the project, instead of working as a regular employee for a single employer.

gig economy A labor market characterized by short-term contract and freelance work.

journalism The occupation of collecting, writing, and editing news for presentation in the media.

marketing An industry that promotes services or products through targeted methods of communicating with the public.

media Mass communication, usually associated with news, that includes publishing, broadcasting, and the internet.

monetize To earn money from a business venture.

plagiarism The act of presenting someone else's words or ideas as one's own.

portfolio A collection of a person's best creative work, organized to display his or her skills, especially to a prospective employer.

press release A statement or announcement of a newsworthy item that is distributed to the press, often to generate publicity.

proofread To read and mark corrections in a piece of writing.

proposal The formal suggestion or presentation of a plan, scheme, or idea.

query An inquiry, usually in the form of a letter, from a writer to an editor proposing a story, article, or book idea.

résumé A written outline and description of a person's educational and professional qualifications and experience.

revenue The income produced by a given source.

self-published Published and distributed
   independently by the author.
social media Networking websites and digital
   applications where users create and share their
   content.
technical writing Writing that focuses on
   instruction about a particular subject.

FURTHER READING

Books:

Burling, Alexis. *Working in Writing*. Mankato, MN: 12 Story Library, 2018.

Cuban, Mark, Ian McCue and Shaan Patel. *Kid Start-Up: How You Can Be An Entrepreneur.* New York, NY: Diversion Books, 2018.

Green, Robert. *Careers If You Like Writing.* San Diego, CA: ReferencePoint Press, Inc., 2017.

Martin, Steve. *Entrepreneur Academy.* London, UK: Ivy Kids, 2018.

O'Phelan, Ann Marie. *The Young Adult's Guide to Selling Your Art, Music, Writing, Photography & Crafts Online: Turn Your Hobby into Cash.* Ocala, FL: Atlantic Publishing Group, Inc., 2017.

Owen, Ruth. *I Can Start a Business!* New York, NY: Rosen Publishing, 2018.

Pelos, Rebecca and Greg Roza. *Cool Careers Without College for People Who Love Writing and Blogging.* New York, NY: Rosen Publishing, 2018.

Sutherland, Adam. *Be A Young Entrepreneur.* London, UK: Wayland Publishers, 2018.

Websites:

Digital.com

digital.com/blog/young-entrepreneurs

This mentorship site offers young entrepreneurs thorough help for starting and growing a successful business.

Entrepreneur.com

Entrepreneurs can get advice for starting a business at every level.

GoTeenWriters.com

Run by young authors, this community-based site helps young writers find support through a variety of resources and hands-on encouragement.

TheWriteLife.com

A one-stop shop for writers that offers guidance, writing development, and connections to writing opportunities.

BIBLIOGRAPHY

"24 Awesome Jobs for Writers That Offer Real Opportunities." Trade-Schools.Net, accessed April 2, 2019. www.trade-schools.net/articles /jobs-for-writers.asp#jobs-for-writers.

Bamidele. "23 Quick Actions You Can Do Today to Make Money Writing." Writers In Charge, accessed April 3, 2019. www.writersincharge. com/actions-to-make-money-writing.

Business Advice. "Young and Mighty: How 14-year-old Henry Patterson is teaching children to embrace entrepreneurship." May 18, 2018. businessadvice.co.uk/on-the-up/young- mighty-henry-patterson-not-before-tea -children-entrepreneurship.

Cattanach, Jamie. "Want to Make Money Blogging as a Teenager? Yes, It's Possible." The Write Life, May 1, 2017. thewritelife.com/make-money -blogging-as-a-teenager.

De Vise, Daniel. "Teens Tutor Teens at Student -Created Firm." *Washington Post*, September 7, 2008. Accessed April 15, 2019. www. washingtonpost.com/wp-dyn/content/ article/2008/09/06/AR2008090602881.html.

King, Stephen. *On Writing: A Memoir of the Craft*. 10th anniversary ed. New York, NY: Scribner, 2010.

Lemire, Timothy. *I'm an English Major—Now What? How English Majors Can Find Happiness, Success, and a Real Job.* Cincinnati, OH: Writer's Digest Books, 2006.

My Baba. "Britain's Youngest Author & Entrepreneur Henry Patterson on Business, Writing and Richard Branson." April 7, 2015. www.mybaba.com/britains-youngest-author -entrepreneur-henry-patterson-on-business -writing-and-richard-branson.

Peer2Peer Tutors LinkedIn. "About Us." LinkedIn. com, accessed April 10, 2019. www.linkedin. com/company/peer2peer-tutors.

Phillpott, Siôn. "The 9 Most Successful Teen Entrepreneurs in the World (2018)." CareerAddict.com, November 14, 2015. www. careeraddict.com/teen-entrepreneurs.

Teen Ink. "Peer Tutoring—Teen Community Service Essay." Accessed April 10, 2019. www. teenink.com/hot_topics/community_service /article/4065/Peer-Tutoring.

Thomson Reuters. "Reporting and Writing Basics—Handbook of Journalism." Accessed April 10, 2019. handbook.reuters.com/index. php/Reporting_and_Writing_Basics.

Wiehardt, Ginny. "Publications for Young Writers—Young Writers Publish Their Creative Writing." The Balance Careers, January 25, 2018. www.thebalancecareers.com/publications-for -young-writers-1277409.

Yager, Fred, and Jan Yager. *Career Opportunities in the Publishing Industry*. 2nd ed. New York, NY: Checkmark Books, 2010.

INDEX